Potential*ing*
your child in soccer

A parents guide for helping kids maximize their potential in soccer and in life

Dr. Lee Hancock & Robin Russell

Table of Contents

Preface

Preface

We recognize the value of parents and their contribution to Youth Sports and especially Youth Soccer across the world. Without parent involvement and the billions of dollars, euros and pounds they invest in North America and Europe – millions of children would not be able to play organized soccer. This book is for those parents of boys and girls who enjoy soccer and would like to use soccer as a means of personal development for their child.

Most discussions concerning parents in soccer tend to start with how to control the 'problems' that parents might bring to the table. These discussions tend to center around things such as sideline behavior on match days, inappropriate advice given at or before training, or any myriad of suggestions from parents to coach on behalf of little Jonny or Jill. We think these are a symptom of parents not being fully engaged and in the absence of a suggested role they engage in these behaviors. Interestingly instead of educating parents, clubs hold parent meetings at the beginning of the year to deal with these problems by telling parents what they can't do and/or discuss contracts regarding consequences of poor parent conduct.

In this book we take a different approach. We educate. We talk about the positive impact you can have with your behavior. We talk about things you can do every day to engage your child and use their sport experience as a positive building block for their future.

Throughout this book "soccer" is used as a medium for developing potential. Soccer is a competitive place to succeed, fail, improve, assist others, lead, follow, and ultimately, an opportunity to reach potential. The outcome of soccer may have specific achievements but overall the biggest achievement will be for your child to realize how to develop his/her own potential – regardless of the level that is achieved. It will be for us as parents to realize what a powerful, active role we can have in this process of developing potential. So, as you read this book, think about this idea of developing potential in anything your children do and think about how you can play a major role in their development as people.

Also, as you read this book there are a couple of things to keep in mind. 1) We understand that each of you as parents, are in a different place in terms of your child's age and soccer development. While reading this book there may be times when the ideas are best suited for a younger child whereas other ideas are more suited to an older child. 2) While we wrote the book for parents of both genders we understand that some ideas may be better for girls and some ideas best suited for boys.

Thank you for allowing us to be part of the process with you and your child. Between the two authors we have over 60 years experience in education and in soccer. Dr. Lee Hancock is not only a sport psychology consultant for US Soccer and Major League Soccer clubs, but is a father of three boys. Robin Russell has over 40 years experience in soccer education in schools, the English Football Association and since 2005 as the Football Educational Consultant for UEFA. Because we have this experience we realize we don't have all the answers. As a result we want this to be more than just a book, we want it to be a jumping off point to discuss best practices between parents. We have included a number of features in the book designated by icons. The icons relate to tasks and questions 🖊, take home messages ⬆, information or facts ⓘ, case studies 🔎 and recommended web links @.

We would like to start you off by getting you to think about these 3 questions:

- Question #1: Have you asked your children - Why do THEY like to play soccer?
- Question #2: Have you asked yourself – Why do YOU want them to continue playing?
- Question #3: Why do kids QUIT youth sports?
- For discussions surrounding these topics from other soccer parents, visit www.potentialing.com.

In addition, we also provide free access to 4 Soccer Parent e-learning courses via this book. These would have cost you $29.97 but are available FREE through your purchase of this book. To take advantage of this offer, go to www.sportspath.com, click on the left hand column and on the registration page insert these logins:

- E-mail: SoccerParent
- Password: Potentialing

Over 50,000 soccer parents have enrolled in these courses since they were launched in 2007. The courses are the most popular e-learning course for soccer parents and are endorsed and used by many State and National Associations including CAL SOUTH, the California (South) Soccer Association, Massachusetts Youth Soccer Association, New York West, PA West, Illinois, Tennessee and a number of US Youth Soccer Clubs.

Section 1– Potentialing™

Chapter 1 - Potentialing™ – The Act of Developing Potential

Potentialing™ *– is the deliberate process of maximizing someone's possible, yet to be realized, skills and abilities.* It is something parents can do to ensure that their child's soccer experience is a place for growth – both as a person and an athlete. Potentialing is more than just teaching or parenting, it is each of these but much more. It is a balance between our biggest role of simply being "there" as parents and this additional role of helping them, from a parental vantage point, not a coaching one, reach their "possible" skills and abilities. It is an action verb and if done properly it goes to the essence of great teaching and parenting to help kids reach their potential.

Potential is "a hidden, or "yet to be realized", ability that may *or may not* be developed." What this indicates is that if we are describing someone with potential we are saying that they, and their yet-to-be-reached skill set, are a possibility. These possible skills and abilities are, one can assume, what we as parents want our kids to reach - with their efforts and, of course for the purposes of this book, with our efforts as well. If this is the case then wouldn't we want our actions and words to support this process of potentialing? But is this the action or behavior we exhibit at games and trainings or the way we approach conversations with our children about their sport?

Think about it, when you are attending your child's games, are you potentialing? Are your actions and behaviors helping your child reach his or her skills and abilities...or are your behaviors pushing them away from reaching these things? Are you too wrapped up in ensuring they win the game or get their chance to be the next Messi or Ronaldo?

This is a look in the mirror moment. When you are attending your child's games are you yelling at the referee? Are you yelling at your child during the game? Are you shaking your head as they make a mistake – so that they look at you and you know that they see you? Do you get your child in the car and discuss their performance – often with you talking and him/her listening? Do you make comments like how could you do that or that was awful? Is this potentialing? Not likely, this is emoting and frequently satisfying your own needs vs. that of your child.

The commitment to potentialing changes the expectations and role of a parent in this developmental process. We understand that parenting, and in this case soccer parenting and developing skills and abilities, does not come with a manual. Many coaches suggest that the best thing a parent can do is just be positive or stay out of the way of children as they move through their soccer experience. We believe that the parent can play a role that helps develop all the benefits soccer has to offer, from values to quality skills and abilities. Following are a few things we believe potentialing for parents is and is not.

Potentialing is not coaching. Part of the art of potentialing as a parent, as you will see in the following chapters, is to ensure you let the coach be the coach. However, being a sport parent also doesn't have to mean that we just sit there and say nothing. As we will see throughout the book, there are plenty of things we can do as soccer parents, through our potentialing, that help our child learn valuable lessons to ensure they are maximizing their skills and abilities.

Potentialing – and reaching potential - is not an absolute. That is to say there is no end point or definitive – "my child has or has not reached the potential that was set in stone for him or her to reach." Everybody's potential is different and in many senses limitless. So, as you read the book understand that as long as you are creating a great environment, then you are moving them toward reaching their skills and abilities, whatever they might be.

Potentialing is an opportunity to strengthen the relationship you have with your child. For you it is a process of learning what it takes to be a great sport parent. It is a quest to engage in a positive process to move your child along a continuum. For the child it is an opportunity to learn to involve you as a parent as he or she learns the game. For you both it is an opportunity to be involved in your child's development as a team vs. as adversaries, so that you two can grow as a unit well into the child's future.

Potentialing in one area can lead to real confidence in other areas of life. As we seek to help our kids develop their skills and abilities, this process; this arduous, difficult, rewarding, fun-filled process, will show the child their efforts lead to improvements. These improvements are the backbone of self-confidence. This confidence that has been developed shows this kid that they can indeed do it and if they can do it here maybe they can do it somewhere else if they go about this same process, with of course you as their most staunch and active supporter.

Potentialing understands that helping someone reach his or her potential is a gradual process. Potential is not reached overnight. Children have many twists and turns and unexpected things that affect their development. Sometimes it appears that children are moving toward their potential and sometimes it may appear that they are moving away from it. As a parent, it is our role in this potentialing process to understand that we gradually help our children reach their potential with our words and actions.

But how do we know how to move our children along this journey, this process? How much is too much? How little is too little? The truth is there is no concrete formula, but we do have a plan.

Potentialing requires a plan. Our plan centers around the creation of a great environment. We use the *Big 5* to discuss how to create this environment. The *Big 5* are a set of developmental pieces organized and presented to you in such a way as to help you engage in potentialing with your son or daughter. Basically what we do is show you how to use the medium of **Play** and the skills of **Communication** to drive forward your child's **Confidence, Persistence and Motivation.** If we can show you the benefits of the *Big 5* – through quality descriptions of the concepts, ideas on roles and responsibilities, real life scenarios, and small examples about well-known professionals and their parents – then we believe we can show you how to engage in potentialing with your children.

Take home message – Potentialing is the deliberate process of developing someone's possible, yet to be realized, skills and abilities. Potentialing can range from just being there as a parent to providing an idea that helps your child improve. Potentialing is a process and a journey with and for your child and there is no absolute or set place that they are supposed to get to as they progress. More than anything else, potentialing is an opportunity to create a great environment with and for your child in order to help them reach their potential.

Notes:

_____

_____

_____

_____

_____

_____

_____

_____

_____

_____

_____

_____

_____

_____

_____

_____

_____

_____

_____

_____

_____

_____

_____

_____

_____

_____

Section 2 – Defining the Potentialing Environment

Chapter 2 – The Big 5: The Importance of a Great Environment

The environment can make all the difference in the development of "potentiality" into "actuality". But just what are we talking about when we say "environment"? The environment for a youth player is any physical or social setting where they are learning or developing. This "environment" is created by coaches, teammates, and of course parents. It can be a competitive practice environment where the coach has put the child in what they feel is a must win situation, a critical game environment where a child's every move is being scrutinized by peers or coaches, or a car ride home after game where the parent says to the child did you have fun and did you work hard. But, then, what is an example of a <u>great</u> environment?

Lets look at an example of a great environment in something we as parents can likely all relate to, a classroom. It would seem that a great environment in a classroom would be one where our child learns what they need to learn and enjoys the process of learning. Where they take the initiative for their own learning by working on their own. Where they ask questions, solve problems, improve, make mistakes, learn from those mistakes, and in general gain a real confidence so that they can use this information throughout their life. The flip side of this would be an environment where the child does not learn what they need to because they were scared to take chances for fear of being ridiculed, where they hated doing homework, didn't ever do things without being asked to do them and in general were so non-confident that they just said, "forget it, I don't want to do this." Many of us have, unfortunately, seen the second example more often than the first.

But just what might happen (or for some of us has already happened) as a result of being in that one great environment as described above? One that was ripe with opportunities to ask questions, solve problems, make mistakes, get rewarded, get challenged and so on and so on. This could not only spark initial interest and desire because of the way the environment was set up but that spark may turn into a burning fire that yearns for more and more opportunities to be challenged and find success.

A parent involved in their child's soccer experience can create and nurture this same spark by creating a great environment. The spark can be nurtured and grown by daily occurrences that feed the child their daily dose of quality interactions that occur as they participate in soccer. The truth is that the environment a parent creates surrounding their child's soccer experience can make all the difference as children develop and realize their skills and abilities.

Claudio Reyna – *A Great Environment*

Claudio Reyna is considered by many to be one of the best soccer players the United States has ever produced. Reyna, born to a Portuguese-American mother and an Argentine-American father, had a stellar professional career for clubs such as Bayer Leverkusen, Wolfsburg, Sunderland, Rangers of Scotland and Manchester City of the English Premiere league before ending his career with the New York Red Bulls in 2008.

By all accounts Claudio grew up in a home that provided an encouraging environment that helped him develop as a player and as a person. Reyna's father, who was also a professional player, espoused the virtues of hard work and humility as Claudio honed in his soccer skills. "He always loved the soccer," Miguel Reyna said. "He liked playing so much, from 4 or 5 years old. He played in our backyard every day, and would kick the ball against the wall. He would practice long passes."

Claudio said about his father that "he worked me hard and was demanding, but in the right way." Claudio also said that his father told him "to respect my job and to play as hard as I can." Adding that when he played it was "good to talk to him, two or three times a week" and that he was the first guy he spoke with after a game.

Now Claudio, himself a parent, espouses the same virtues he grew up with. "More than anything, I like being a good role model and leading by example." "And it's great being their guide, letting them find things on their own rather than controlling them."

http://articles.nydailynews.com/1998-05-31/sports/18069193_1_claudio-reyna-miguel-reyna-soccer

http://www.nyc.gov/html/hra/nycdads/html/notable/notable.shtml

What Makes a Great Soccer Environment?

A great soccer environment should be a lot like the one we described above in a classroom. It is an environment that should be filled with opportunities to enjoy, improve, solve problems, make mistakes, get rewarded, get challenged and so on and so on. But of course we should think about how we can do our part as parents to ensure this environment exists for our child to develop his or her abilities.

This section is written to provide you as parents with information on what concepts you can use to create a great environment for your children throughout their soccer experience. You will see below that we have organized important information into 5 categories – our *Big 5*. The concepts Play, Confidence, Persistence, Motivation and Communication by themselves are important, but put together make up the unique approach of potentialing that we set forth.

As we say in the beginning - basically what we do is show you how to use the *medium* of **Play** and the *skills* of **Communication** to drive forward your child's **Confidence, Persistence and Motivation.** You will see that as we describe one area (such as persistence) it may rely on another (such as communication) to push forward with your child. For example, we explain persistence…and if we can help you help your child persist then we are also building their confidence in the process. If we build their persistence and confidence then we are building their intrinsic motivation to be great. These things together help to make up a great environment for potentialing!

Notes:

Chapter 3 – Play

The initial goal of any child's soccer experience should be that it is enjoyable. Yet somewhere along the way, we, as a parent and child unit, seem to lose our way. The truth is that even for our kids with "potential" - if they are not enjoying it there is very little chance that they will 1) continue to pursue soccer now and as a result 2) very little chance they will reach their potential as a result of not accomplishing 1).

Mia Hamm – *It's About Play*

The retired American forward Mia Hamm is the second most capped female player in soccer history. Her brother played sports, which was the incentive for her to follow the same path. Mia played a lot of pickup games with her older brother and his friends. Opposing bigger, stronger, faster players bettered her stamina and contributed to her technical abilities.

Her father – Bill Hamm, coached the team where Mia played, when she was 10-11 years old. He shares their experience and he advices the parents to give their children the freedom in the decision to pursue a soccer career. "She got tired of playing soccer for some reason. So, she took a break for one of the seasons. She sat back for about six months. In the next season, she returned with new enthusiasm and a desire to play. She had recharged her batteries and wanted to play soccer again," says Bill Hamm.

Mia herself also shares the same opinion on her desire to play because she wanted to play not because someone else wanted her to play. "My parents really allowed soccer - and whatever I chose - to be my passion and not theirs."

http://en.wikipedia.org/wiki/Mia_Hamm

http://www.socceramerica.com/article/46323/mia-hamms-advice-for-girls-parents-and-coaches.html

Think about some of the things that you are very good at and are passionate about improving. It is likely that those things that you have chosen to pursue, with passion and fervor, are those that you enjoy. They don't seem like work...even though your passion may also in fact be your work. In fact, if we can try to ensure children approach this endeavor with a mindset of <u>playing soccer vs. working soccer</u> then we have already helped set a direction.

The word that describes what people do with the game of soccer is not work or drudge or even attempt, it is play. Most everyone can agree that play is inherently fun and exciting. More importantly for us as parents though, is that play and enjoyment will be critical determinants in how often, how long and with what force children currently engage in, and continue to engage in, soccer.

Kids are involved in sports for a variety of reasons - to experience excitement, receive awards, win games, or be physically fit. However, the number one reason children are involved in sports is to have fun. The top two reasons children drop out of sport are that they are not having any fun and that they lost interest. We can clearly see that keeping a child's environment enjoyable and stimulating is a key factor for their desire to participate. Of course making it enjoyable doesn't mean it is always easy but it does mean that children, in order to remain interested, need to see that they are playing soccer not working soccer.

With this in mind we will ask that **you begin your potentialing by viewing your son's or daughter's soccer direction through "play-colored glasses."** Meaning, let's use the idea of playing soccer vs. working soccer as the basic cornerstone of how we watch, and talk to them about, their soccer experience. Don't get us wrong here, we realize the competition and hardness of the game, but let's face it, when some of the best tough midfielders or center backs get into a tackle, it looks fun and they look like they enjoy it. Moreover, when you see players put years into perfecting whatever it is they are known for being good at (Drogba backing into players, Messi weaving in and out of players, Scholes picking out passes, etc.), you know that there must have been some real enjoyment in their pursuit for greatness.

Take home message – Play should be the context, the lens that shapes our potentialing approach. Play should provide us a basic foundation as we move through this process of potentialing. Meaning, whenever we get bogged down in the game we should be able to return to this basic premise and remember how to make it a game again, how to get our children to enjoy playing soccer vs. working soccer.

As we said above, children begin and continue to play soccer because it is enjoyable. We asked you to look at your child's play through play colored glasses and to get your child to play soccer vs. work soccer. But why is this important? Why might this help develop potential into real quality?

Below we explain some key theories that explain why play is so important in the development of ability. These theories, while in some cases are complex, provide a much needed foundation for us to go forward. At the end of each theory we try to get to the essence of the information in our "take home messages" so it is useable for you and your child.

Common Theories of Play and Characteristics of Play

Theories on play will serve to help us see why enjoyment and play have a major impact on early learning and development. Also, characteristics identified as key factors that happen during play are actually equally as important to being an elite athlete. Simply put, there are some things that happen in play that help kids enjoy things more and as a result lay a solid foundation for what it means to be a great athlete. Here are 3 key theories or factors in play.

Piaget's Theory – Piaget suggested that children progress through a series of cognitive stages during which their thought processes become increasingly similar to an adults.

In order to move through these steps, children need to play and learn and play and learn, etc. While play is not at the heart of this particular theory, Piaget would argue that children need to have the opportunity to practice and combine acquired skills in order for them to be part of their new reality and their new skill set. For us, an example would be a child that has just learned a certain type of pass or move. If they aren't allowed to enjoy this and use it in an environment focused on play then the likelihood of your child making this part of their repertoire in games going forward is unlikely.

Take home message from Piaget – Let kids have the chance to play and try new skills free from judgment and under their own volition.

Vygotsky's Theory – Lev Vygotsky essentially believes play helps kids develop their ability to think. He also believes that play helps kids develop their social and emotional skills and believes these domains are interrelated. Play is a tool that children use to help themselves learn about and make sense of new things and concepts.

He talks about this "zone of proximal development" (ZPD), which is a combination between a child's *actual development* (meaning what he or she has actually been able to do) and his or her *potential development* (what he or she may be able to do).

Potential development in the ZPD is a transitional state in which kids need scaffolding to makes sense, in this case new sense, of what they are doing. Scaffolding in this case is very much like scaffolding that construction workers would need to reach a higher place on a building, but for children this scaffolding is created and used by them. This *potential development* phase, and this scaffolding, is created by the child as they play with objects or with items or with others and stretches their development in areas such as self control, cooperation, memory and of course ability.

Think about it – a child is playing with a toy car. Through trial and error, the child figures out that this car can actually roll twice as fast when he pulls it back then pushes it. Then he also figures out that it goes even faster when it goes down steps and it also serves to move a lot of his other toys around as a moving vehicle and so on and so on. The child can stop and start his play episode whenever he wants, suspend reality and basically do whatever he wants in this scenario as it is his play episode. The child has manipulated his own transitional state, his own *potential development* and made it his own *actual development* all by his own power.

Vygotsky believed that this safe place to try out new skills is important in cognitive and emotional development because it was a safe place to try them out before it got to any formal areas such as school or sport.

Take home message - Vygotsky would say, let the kids mess around with the ball. Put your child in a place where they can use some of their own scaffolding in this potential development phase to build some new skills. If you can do this they will likely feel like they have built these skills themselves and as a result are more happy and confident.

Set up times for your child to play – with you and without you. Can you kick it around with your child against a wall? Can you find your child some chances to play with some friends at the park? The truth is the more chances you provide your child with an opportunity to "play" the more likely Vygotsky's theory has a chance to come to fruition.

To summarize - children can learn to scaffold on their own, building necessary connections as they play.

Characteristics of Play – Garvey identified "dispositional" factors that are observed during play. These "dispositional" factors are basically things that happen to kids as they play. We include these to show the reader how important play is in the development of the child and their pursuit of their potential.

Characteristics include:

1. Intrinsic motivation – Kids are doing the activity because they want to do it not because they are told to do it. This internal desire helps kids excitement levels and provides an opportunity to continue to do it because they want to do it (Intrinsic motivation is #2 of our *Big 5*.) but also helps develop a healthy persistence (persistence is #3 in our *Big 5*).

2. Process (vs. product) orientation - Kids focus on improving and getting better as opposed to purely achieving a result. Meaning, as kids play they make mistakes, when they make mistakes there is an opportunity to stop or try again. But if they are playing and attempting to get better, mistakes are just an opportunity to try again. This is a key component in one of our *Big 5* - that of developing persistence (#3) and obviously can lead to greater confidence over time as a result (#4).

3. Positive affect – when kids play they enjoy what they are doing. This is important, as we want to ensure that children approach their soccer practice and games with a sense of pleasure and enjoyment. If we can help with this approach then we can hopefully help the child with this positive affect that they will get as they are playing soccer.

Take home message - These characteristics of play are actually seen in kids as they play and of course this is important as these characteristics form the basis for a child's motivation, persistence, and confidence in our Big 5.

Chapter take home message - Again, the idea behind this chapter is that as we are potentialing we should help our children continue to enjoy "play"ing soccer vs. working soccer as it is helpful in creating this great environment. The truth is that people need to play to get it right. Recall the take home messages from Piaget and Vygotsky – kids need time to mess around with the soccer ball in order that they get better and can apply some of the moves they've learned. Think about it, has any creative techie ever built the perfect device on the first try? Or better yet, with their supervisor right on top of them? No chance, the techie was probably left alone to play with his toys and voilà - iPhone!! Well maybe not iPhone but you get the idea here. And of course Garvey shows that when kids play they actually reveal certain characteristics – these characteristics are not just important for children but also for elite athletes.

Notes:

_____

_____

_____

_____

_____

_____

_____

_____

_____

_____

_____

_____

_____

_____

_____

_____

_____

_____

_____

_____

_____

_____

_____

_____

_____

Chapter 4 – Motivation

How do you like to be told what to do? You don't like it?
Neither do kids. The truth is that while sometimes being told
what to do gets "stuff" done the most productive "stuff" and
most meaningful "stuff" is done when you want to do it. It's not
to say that sometimes children don't need to be told what to do,
they of course do. BUT do they need to be told to play...to play
soccer? Yes, we sometimes have to push our kids to do
something that we know they need to do and if they don't do it
they may fall behind; but if we push them too much, they will
quit...this is one of those key times in potentialing.

The right amount of extrinsic (other people or rewards)
motivation and intrinsic (the desire from within) motivation is
key. Can kids be successful by just someone/something else
pushing them? Is it more beneficial if they do it on their own?
(Obvious answer here). And is there some way that we can get
them to want to do it on their own? We will look at these
questions below and talk about how we can build that desire
from within.

Henrik Larsson – *Watch and Learn…To Be Motivated*

Henrik Larsson, renowned as possibly the best Swedish football player of all time, attributes his love for soccer to his father. He is the one who gave him a football when Henrik was only 16 months old. Later the future star practiced together with his brothers and friends on a large field near his home in Helsingborg.

His father used to watch a TV program, which introduced the game to Larsson. "We always used to watch football. We had this program in Sweden where they showed English games every Saturday. I used to sit up with him and watch European Cups, World Cups, European Championships, the Swedish National Team. We watched it all," says the former player of Celtic, Barcelona and Manchester United.

At an early age Henrik's father gave him a video of Pelé's life story, which also inspired him to become a footballer. "If you look at Pele, he could score goals but he could also set up a goal. He has always been my idol."

The first game he saw was in Helsingborg, Sweden. He saw the first international club team, Watford, coming to Heslingborg. Again, his dad took Henrik to watch soccer games.

http://en.wikipedia.org/wiki/Henrik_Larsson
http://www.imdb.com/name/nm1418875/bio
http://www.thecelticwiki.com/page/Larsson,+Henrik

Extrinsic Motivation - That Little Something Else

Extrinsic motivation refers to the performance of an activity in order to attain some benefit as a result of participation. When people are externally motivated they participate in an activity because it is a means to some end, perhaps a trophy or money, rather than for the sake of participation in the activity itself. Now of course this is sometimes a good thing.

Kids need things to strive for and being motivated by the attainment of these "things" is often very helpful. Think about it, when there is concrete recognition of achievement, such as a trophy or some other reward, this can be a powerful motivator. These incentives can serve to spark a child's interest. But these can also be detrimental. If these things are provided by a parent, in the form of $1 per goal, a special meal if they win, etc... kids may come to expect this or something more as life progresses. Remember play is intrinsic and while playing soccer may carry some extrinsic rewards, we want those to be things the child earns/brings up on their own vs. something you provide. Over time if the pursuit of something else is the only thing that's there, it can be detrimental: because what happens if they get "it"?

What happens if they sign a contract at 14? Now what? Is this the pinnacle? The truth is, that kids, if they are purely extrinsically motivated, will struggle. They may experience higher stress and anxiety and when push comes to shove may cheat to get what they want and/or quit. But the good news is that we have other motivations that are also at play...it will be our job as parents to manage their extrinsic motivation and enhance their intrinsic motivation.

Take home message – Extrinsic motivation can be a key piece in potentialing. But for kids with passion it is often there already. The key will be to manage this extrinsic motivation over time and ensure their intrinsic desire is there as well. We will address how to do this below.

Intrinsic Motivation

Intrinsic motivation refers to performing an activity for the sake of the activity itself. When an individual is intrinsically motivated he or she is involved in the activity purely for the satisfaction or joy of the activity or to learn something or improve. Think about it, play is intrinsic. When kids love what they are doing they are more likely to do more of it. If kids are to reach their potential they will need to do more of whatever it is they want to excel at. So the trick is how do we get them to want to do it on their own. The truth is we can't. BUT, if, in our potentialing endeavors, we create the right environment that focuses on some important variables, we most surely can create a place where we are fostering their intrinsic motivation.

There is a major theory from children's sport and education called self-determination theory. Basically it says that the more a teacher coach or parent focuses on building some essential needs that children have, the more the child will participate in the activity because they want to vs. because they are told to...so for intrinsic reasons. These 3 needs are competence, autonomy and relatedness.

Competence simply means that the child feels that he or she is good at the skill. The goal of the parent, if they are to improve intrinsic motivation, is to help the child feel that they are competent at the task at hand. Of course this is not done overnight and with constant praise, especially if something has not been done well.

This is built on many conversations over a long period of time where the child a) learns what it means to be competent (so learns to judge their own skill and be honest with themselves) and b) the parent learns to communicate effectively with their child at appropriate times (see communication chapter below and specific scenarios). This is a good place to remind ourselves that as children develop there are many twists and turns and yes a child may feel that they are not competent sometimes and this may be a good thing as long as we are positively encouraging them through these trying times.

Autonomy means how much *choice* the child feels he or she has in regards to the task. When someone feels like they have some choice in what they are doing they have more control. This control provides anyone, and specifically here the child, with some much-needed personal input into perhaps what, when, how long, etc. they are doing something. In essence what we are talking about here is that if the child feels like they have some choice in their soccer than they are likely to improve their intrinsic motivation. But what sort of choice and how much is appropriate?

Kristine Lilly – *Choices Are Key*

Kristine Lilly, the world record holder for national team appearances with 352, debuted for the USA at age 16 in 1987 and retired in 2010 at age 39. She is veteran of five World Cups and three Olympic games. She shares that her family opened the door of sport for her. "We were a very sports-oriented family. On weekends, sports were on TV. Football, any sport … bowling, baseball. We'd always have sports on."

Her family has always been a big influence on her career, being very supportive. "They've allowed me to try everything and basically said, "This is your world; do what you want." Kristine says that her parents also contributed to the building of her winning mentality. They encouraged her to risk with decisions. They only demanded that she fulfill her commitments; encouraging her to finish what she starts and not to give up.

http://en.wikipedia.org/wiki/Kristine_Lilly

http://www.socceramerica.com/article/47290/kristine-lilly-good-coaches-create-good-memories.html

The truth is there is no magic pill in regards to how much choice to provide. But if we provide children with opportunities for choice within their required play times (trainings, games, seasons) this will increase their intrinsic motivation. In addition, if we provide opportunities for the child to have extra play times (against the wall, at the park, with friends, with you, etc.) in the game and they choose to do it, this is a good thing. The more these times occur the more intrinsic motivation is apparent...and this too is a good thing.

Relatedness is how much someone feels they are a part of a group. If the child feels that they are part of a group than they are likely to increase their intrinsic motivation. But which group...team, friends, other?

The truth is there can be many groups that the child may want to feel a part of that may impact their intrinsic motivation. The one that we as a parent group can impact is the parent child group.

Normally relatedness refers to how related the child feels to the group that they are involved with in the sport. But it would stand to reason that if the child felt *related* to you – if they were able to feel that you were on their team, in their corner and part of this quest for your child to reach their potential they would feel this cohesive group connection with you. If this were the case they would feel related to this group of you and them and it would likely increase their motivation. But how do we do this? We will explore detailed scenarios in chapter 11 but the truth is that this is built on real conversations at key times over a long period of time.

Chapter take home message - Intrinsic motivation is vital if a child is truly going to be great at what they do. Intrinsic motivation ignites this passion in a child and pushes them to want to be great...on their own.

As parents we can do our part in potentialing by fostering competence, autonomy and relatedness. Of course there are key times and key ways to do this, as we will see in the scenarios chapter. And as we will see, if we have the intrinsic motivation, we are also developing the child's inner desire to continue to improve in the face of difficult times...we are developing their persistence!

Notes:

Chapter 5 – Persistence

So how are motivation and persistence different? They truly do go hand and hand but there are some major differences as we engage in our potentialing efforts. For our purposes we wanted to separate these two because of the amount of opportunities for failure in sport. That's right, failure.

As we said earlier, soccer is a great place to fail and succeed ALL the time. So, we can have a young player who is very intrinsically motivated to be successful. They can want to show up to training, try hard, be competent, have choices and enjoy it…but what happens when they lose? What happens when there are real obstacles that they need to overcome in order to move forward?

We feel that you can be extrinsically or intrinsically motivated to do all of these things - but the true measure to reach a person's "possible skills and abilities" is how much someone goes after something in the face of failure. It is this persistence in the face of competition (as you will see below) that can really help the young developing person in their quest to improve. And, more importantly, can help us as we engage in potentialing this young person as they tackle small failures in life.

Here are some fun facts about persistence in order to be great:

The "10,000-Hour Rule" is based on a study by Swedish Psychologist, Anders Ericsson. His research showed that it takes approximately 10,000 hours of deliberate practice to master a skill. 'Deliberate Practice' was defined as really attempting to practice the things you can't master!

Malcolm Gladwell in his book 'Outliers' claims that greatness requires enormous time, using the source of The Beatles' musical talents and Gates' computer savvy as examples. http://en.wikipedia.org/wiki/Outliers_(book) - cite_note-usa-success-2 The Beatles performed live in Hamburg Germany over 1,200 times from 1960 to 1964, amassing more than 10,000 hours of playing time, therefore meeting the 10,000-Hour Rule. Gladwell asserts that all of the time The Beatles spent performing shaped their talent, and quotes Beatles' biographer Phillip Norman as saying, "so by the time they returned to England from Hamburg, Germany, 'they sounded like no one else. It was the making of them.'" Gates met the 10,000-Hour Rule when he gained access to a high school computer in 1968 at the age of 13, and spent 10,000 hours programming on it.

Similar studies point to the value of deliberate practice in developing sporting skills including soccer but while deliberate practice remains absolutely crucial, it's important to remember that the most important skills we develop at an early age are not domain specific. (In other words, Tiger Woods is not using the same golf swing he relied on as a 5 year old.) Instead, the real importance of early childhood has to do with the development of general cognitive and non-cognitive traits, such as self-control, patience, grit, and the willingness to persist. This is also the lesson of a recent study on Australian football players:

The developmental histories of 32 players in the Australian Football League (AFL), independently classified as either expert or less skilled in their perceptual and decision-making skills, were collected through a structured interview process and their year-on-year involvement in structured and deliberate play activities retrospectively determined. Despite being drawn from the same elite level of competition, the expert decision-makers differed from the less skilled in having accrued, during their developing years, more hours of experience in structured activities other than Australian football.

As you can see, when someone is described as persistent there is usually an immediate thought about how hard that person is working, or has worked, to obtain what they were going after. In fact to persist literally means to "continue steadfastly or firmly in some state, purpose, course of action, especially in spite of opposition." These qualities, for someone striving to reach their potential, are in fact vital.

Is your child persistent in the face of adversity? When does it appear as if they are persistent...when they win or when they lose or both? Are they driven, are they competitive? Is being competitive good? These are all things that we need to consider as we engage in potentialing their persistence.

We really should recognize what persistence is actually saying about our child with potential. In fact we see our kids do this all the time, especially our kids with potential. They "continue" very "firmly" with a real "purpose" especially vs. an "opposition"...They compete! Really, when a child is being *persistent* what we are essentially saying is that they are *competing* to be *successful*.

Recall, we said above, it is this steadfast pursuit of something more, some success in the face of some opposition. There is nothing inherently wrong with competition. But for the purposes of our potentialing journey it is of vital importance that we understand 1) just how our children are defining success and who they are competing against and 2) how we are creating the environment so that they learn how to judge their success, compete with a purpose and ultimately persist.

Children engage in competitive endeavors on a daily basis, whether we call attention to it or not. How many times have we seen a child trying to compete in a dribbling game during practice or in a one on one game? During these times children are competing; they are being persistent at the task in order to be *successful*. Now, the important component here, and one that is vital in our potentialing is how these players are judging *success*. It is important because children will *persist* in the face of *competition* more if they perceive success a certain way and if we reward success a certain way.

Tim Cahill– *Competitive And Focused On The Process*

The Australian soccer player Tim Cahill was influenced mostly by his father in his decision to become a soccer player. His father, Tim Cahill Sr., taught him a couple of valuable lessons that football had to be fun, but to be good you had to work at technique and compete hard.

Tim Cahill is competitive, but his biggest goal as he competes appears to be relative to himself and his improvement. "The drive to do well comes from within," says Cahill. Cahill describes that when he doesn't play well he looks at himself first and what he could have done better in his preparation, saying "there is a reasoning when I haven't played well, so I question my self, my diet, whether I've slept well, and I feel after reflecting on the weeks training I can say it is because of A, B, or C."

The Australian international describes how hard he competed - with himself - especially if people said he wasn't good enough or didn't work hard enough. He says "People saying I wasn't good enough, wasn't strong enough, or too small. That pushed me forward; that gave me an added incentive."

He also described how he focused on the process of improvement, even after people gave him complements. He said "the first thing I think is I've got to train harder tomorrow, I've got to play better, I need to find the next level."

http://en.wikipedia.org/wiki/Tim_Cahill_(footballer)http://www.imdb.com/name/nm2169232/bio

http://www.theage.com.au/news/Soccer/Brothers-in-arms/2004/11/27/1101495458292.html?from=moreStories

http://www.theaustralian.com.au/archive/sportold/tim-cahill-chases-dream/story-fn4l4sip-1225867179209

Achievement goal theory is commonly used by sport researchers to investigate and explain children's competitive approaches in sport. The theory basically states that kids think in two ways. If they are process oriented they are focused on improving and learning and judge success relative to their own improvement. If they are product oriented they are focused on winning and beating others and judge that they are successful when they beat others; and conversely feel like they are a failure if they lose. The truth is that the best athletes in the world are both. But if kids are too much *product* and not enough *process* then when the going gets tough, they quit as they get anxious and have no coping skills or desire to improve or to learn what it takes to win….in other words they do not persist. The next part of this theory is where parents come in.

The theory also says that parents and coaches create climates that reward success during competition in one of two ways. Some parents (and coaches) create a product environment and stress winning/beating others above all else. They say, "did you win," or "if you did not win you are a failure" (extreme example but it happens). Or a parent creates a process environment when they stress working/trying hard and where success is measured relative to themselves vs. others. The parent that is constantly stressing the product environment to a product child is saying to the kid, yes, winning is the most important thing. This is fine, as long as the child keeps winning, but they don't. And when they don't, you guessed it, they enjoy it less, they don't persist…they quit.

Take home message - The climate you create is critical in your potentialing. A lot of kids with potential are "product oriented" – basically saying that when they compete they want to win. That is great, there is nothing wrong with wanting to win...BUT they must also have a process oriented approach to cope with the small failures/losses and get better and better – essentially learn to persist. This is where you are key. You can actually change the way a child approaches day to day instances of competition – including how they deal with falling over the ball, missing a pass, losing a one on one game, etc. You can ensure, with your comments and feedback at critical times (which we will address in chapter 7), that they have a healthy approach to their daily activities and ultimately learn how to persist at developing their own potential.

Parents, if we can learn to stress one over another we are potentialing because we are creating an environment of persistence in the face of adversity or competition.

The basic idea is that a parent who stresses things such as trying hard, attempting skills, or getting up after being knocked down will be developing children that believe their success is due to effort (as opposed to innate ability that can't be changed), players that will enjoy the game more, and for the purposes of this *Big 5* component players that will persist (as opposed to those that quit). A parent that stresses winning over everything else will be developing kids that get anxious when things don't initially go their way, get frustrated instead of looking for solutions and will not enjoy it if they do not win and of course will not persist. Striving for a win and discussing winning aren't inherently bad but oftentimes winning is not in your control…especially in soccer.

Here is an example: A young player has early winning success because they are bigger stronger and faster. They don't practice skills but still win. The parent praises the win as opposed to the effort. The child gets to a certain age and loses, repeatedly to a smaller player that lost plenty of times as a younger smaller player but whose parents praised their efforts and encouraged them to continue to practice their skills in the face of losses. As a result the bigger stronger faster child – once push came to shove in this competitive match – had no coping skills, as they always just won…so what do they do? They get a bit anxious, they enjoy it less and they quit (they fail to persist). Whereas the smaller child, even though they just won, still understands that yes winning was great, but there is more to do…they must continue to persist to drive for something more.

Kids compete everyday and some will continue to win – sometimes with ease. But what happens when our child with potential comes up against another with potential? There are two kids with exceptional skill sets that, especially if they are on the same team and practice everyday together, will compete often and win and lose with equal frequency. Will your child persist in the face of adversity or will they quit? This actually gets at the essence of potentialing.

If anyone is to reach their full potential, there will be times that it is tested. If we as a parental unit are stressing these *Big 5* - concept 3 tenets of improve, get better, try your hardest, focus on the process not the product, measure success relative to you vs. others, then we are potentialing. We are creating this environment that says it is the work you put in day in and day out that makes all the difference - even if you are good now. We are stressing these important characteristics that lay the foundation for persistence and a continued drive for an intrinsically motivated player.

The devil will of course be in the detail. That is to say when a win is on the line how will you behave? Will you shake your head in massive frustration when they lose even though they played very well? Will you use the car ride home as a way to engage in potentialing or a way to emote your frustrations? This concept 3 – developing persistence is within your child but can be made or broken by you. If your child is constantly under pressure by you then why would they choose to participate when the pressure is debilitating.

Chapter take home message - The climate you create is critical in your potentialing. Stress these tenets - improve, get better, try your hardest, focus on the process not the product, measure success relative to you vs. others. Learning to win and learning to be great can be your focus as they are under the child's control – vs. winning the game, which often is not.

Developing persistence is a long process and one that should adhere to the same message in all sorts of situations - from the development of individual ball skills where it is just them, to pressure filled games vs. someone else.

Notes:

Chapter 6 – Confidence

You will see that the first 3 of the *Big 5* are relatively short chapters while this one is quite a bit longer. That is because we believe confidence is the holy grail of sports. Meaning when athletes or children have it, no matter what happens, win or lose; they feel great and ready and feel that they can do "it," whatever "it" is, again. And as a result we have a few key areas in here that, when understood and implemented, can make a real impact on the developing child and your potentialing efforts.

When we watch a confident athlete on television or in person, there is this look that they get that says I am great, you know it, I know it and eventually I will prevail. But can you explain exactly what confidence is? Could you tell me why that athlete is confident? More importantly could you tell me how they got that way? Is confidence built or innate...if it can be built how do we build it?

Can confidence be built or is it innate? This one is a tough one as no one can be sure. Most will say it is a combination of both. Sure some people appear naturally confident...but how do we know what happened in their lives up to that point that may have had an impact? To be sure, if you are a teacher or a coach your answer should emphatically be that confidence can be built! What if we told you that confidence can be built and that your potentialing can play a major role in this confidence?

Alex Oxlade-Chamberlain – *Confidence Building*

English talent and Arsenal footballer Alex Oxlade-Chamberlain is the second youngest player with a first team debut for the London club. His father Mark Chamberlain is a former English national footballer. Alex gives recognition to both his parents for his knowledge, development and confidence.

"My mom is a physiotherapist, which is a massive help to me so in terms of nutrition she was the one who made sure I was eating all the right food and I can only thank her that she kept me fit and healthy. When I was younger in pre-season she used to take me out running and doing press-ups. She used to do a bit of training with me until I got a bit too quick for her and she had to cut that out. She's been massive," says the winger.

Arsenal's player has only watched videos of his father's career. But Mark was the first one who gave his son lessons about the physical condition and football techniques. Their games would always end with a sprint; a seven-year-old boy up against his father, a man who just happened to have been one of the quickest professional footballers of his generation. Curiously, the boy would always win, until the day his father decided that his son was ready to know the truth.

"Until I was nine or 10, I genuinely thought I was quicker than him," says Oxlade-Chamberlain, recounting the tale of lost innocence. "Then one day when we raced, he battered me and I didn't know what had happened. Obviously, he thought at that age I could take losing."

At 5ft 11in he is not exactly huge but he is muscular enough to force his way past bigger defenders, although he prefers to beat opponents through technique, calling on skills honed by those sessions in the park with his father. "If I used to take a player on and get away from him, he would catch me up," he explains. "But my dad used to say, "imagine what it'll be like when you're 17 or 18 and you're big and quick. They won't be able to catch you then." If you are a smaller player, you have to use your brain a lot more."

http://www.dailymail.co.uk/sport/football/article-2126621/Alex-Oxlade-Chamberlain-exclusive-The-Year-The-Ox.html#ixzz24kqbS7tC

http://www.dailymail.co.uk/sport/football/article-2126621/Alex-Oxlade-Chamberlain-exclusive-The-Year-The-Ox.html#ixzz24gfL7nkw

http://en.wikipedia.org/wiki/Alex_Oxlade-Chamberlain

We believe confidence can indeed be built. In fact lets work backwards first. Can confidence be torn down? How many times have we ourselves felt great going in to something only for results to not go our way and suddenly doubt creeps into our minds? Suddenly someone that we trust, says to us, "what are you doing, what was that, that is what you are going to do? That is awful!!" Right then and there, confidence – as well as possible motivation, persistence and desire to play – is gone.

Unfortunately, we are sure we have seen this in our child. We perhaps have even negatively impacted their confidence with our words or non-verbal behaviors at practices and games. Have you ever thrown your hands up in disgust during a game – and have they seen you do this? The likely impact of this – depending on the context of the hands up gesture – could be a major confidence blow. Is this potentialing?....No!

Now why would we say work backwards first? Well, because if something can be torn down then why can't it be built up? Why can't these words instead be purposeful potentialing words? The truth is they can.

The likelihood is that we have repeated this process (however inadvertent it may have been for the bad or good) with our children a number of times - both the tearing down and the building up. The important components, and ones that we have already discussed, are that potentialing is 1) methodical and 2) isn't always moving forward. That is to say 1) we must have a sense that every time we say or do something, as it relates to our child's sport experience, it may impact the child, and as a result, we need to know how our words/actions may impact the child. And 2) we understand that a young persons confidence may take 2 steps forward and 1 step back – but this process of 2 forward 1 back can be methodical and thought-filled (not perfect, of course, but as you read the information below, you will hopefully see what we are talking about).

Let's talk about how to engage in potentialing some real confidence in your children. As you will see below, we define a few concepts important to understanding and potentialing confidence. In addition, we reference the sections before this in order to create this deep understanding for you as potentialing parents. Once we set out these concepts the real work will take place in chapter 11 where we throw out some scenarios for you to build their confidence.

Take home message – Confidence can be built. We need to be smart about how we build it as it is OK to fail... meaning sometimes kids will take a confidence hit and be bummed out. It is at these times they need us as a parent first...just to be there NOT to push or prod...just be there; this is also potentialing. Below we talk about how to build confidence, but this is an important point before we go forward.

Defining Confidence

First, let's get a working picture of confidence. The definition of confidence is "belief in ones self or ones abilities" or "full trust, or trustworthiness or reliability of a person or thing." A couple of things in this definition should jump right off the page, namely "belief in self," "trust" and "reliability." For a child to really get at these core components in confidence they will need to start with a quality role model.

The role model is key. As children engage in this sport adventure they will surely be seeing a lot of you. If they see you as a person they can "trust," that they can "rely" on and that "believes in their self" you are setting the tone for them and by the very definition you are building their confidence. Think about it, we as parents can build their initial confidence through our behavior and as a result show them how to behave towards their own behavior – building trust, belief and reliability in themselves.

As an example – a child walks for the first time. Your child sees you see them...you place your hand out as your child walks, they grab it, they fall but you are there...they see that you are smiling and encouraging them. This is a PERFECT example of building confidence. You are building this trust, this reliance, this belief in them as they walk...yes they fall (you may have even let them fall, but falling is part of the process) but you are there. They are learning what it means to have belief and trust in ones self because you are showing them. If they can learn those behaviors from you, surely they can learn to have these in themselves.

Take home message – The power of you. This is one of the most important messages in the book. If you behave in this fashion you are showing them how they should behave towards themselves. They will see first hand what it means to trust in the face of small failures, to be reliable and to believe in ones self (namely them) even if they fall. As we will see below when we talk about "sources of confidence" the components of this definition actually do lay the foundation for day-to-day ways that confidence is built.

Explaining How Confidence Takes Time To Build

Some people think they are good and some people know they are good. The difference is night and day. Think about it, how many teams have we seen, teams that are almost championship caliber? The difference in the approach, demeanor and the championship performance is huge. The want-to-be championship team talks the talk and shows up in some parts of the championship but one or two set backs and they are a bit fulfilled. The truth is that true confidence is built over time and with real experiences...until that time it is that they *think* they are confident they don't *know* they are confident. It takes years for this deep seated REAL confidence to be built. Before that time confidence is TEMPORARY, something that can fluctuate often.

Think of *REAL* confidence as a tree with roots and *TEMPORARY* confidence as a sapling without roots; our job is to help the sapling develop roots. A young tree grows but is frail as its roots are not deep. Any change in climate, temperature, seasons, etc.... will at least impact its growth and at worst knock it over, as its roots have not taken hold. So too it is with a child's *temporary* confidence. When they fail, they may not have these solid confidence roots built up (by you or by them). If this is the case it impacts their confidence and growth, or it may even break their spirit and they may quit. This is a temporary state of confidence, one without deep roots of experience and time ready to weather the storm of criticism and failures.

When the tree gets older it develops roots and is strong. It has developed these roots methodically over the years. It can withstand difficult temperature changes and seasons. In fact in some seasons it may even appear to be struggling (no leaves, etc.) but in fact it is surviving, and while perhaps taking a step back in its appearance, it knows it is ready to come back strong after these difficult times. Once it has "weathered this storm/season" it emerges, stronger than ever and looks the part again.

So too it is with a person's real confidence. This confidence has built up and has grown these roots methodically over the years. It has learned to deal with harsh criticism and difficult times. It knows how to deal with the weather and seasons. Once this real confidence has weathered this storm it re-emerges, as it knew it would, to take its rightful place as this beautiful deep-rooted tree rising in the forest.

It is our potentialing that can help feed and water these *temporary* confidence roots so that they eventually become *real* confidence roots. Of course to build these real confidence roots it takes time, patience and a methodical approach.

Take home message – Build your child's real confidence roots by potentialing their temporary confidence roots. The message here should be simple. Every day is a chance for you to build up a solid foundation for your child's confidence to develop. Sure there will be times where there are tough, honest real conversations where they appear to be taking that step back. But manage those times and understand that timing is everything. We will talk about real scenarios in chapter 11 for how to manage and engage in potentialing their confidence.

But what are these roots of confidence? What are the sources that can help build our child's confidence? Depending on the people we are citing there are 4-10 sources (roots) that build deep self-confidence. For our purposes we will discuss 4 sources that will be the foundation on which we build our tree of confidence.

Sources of Confidence – P.V.S.S. -- The Tree's Roots

Previous successes – have they done it before? The number one way that confidence is built is through previous successes. That is to say, as a child builds up their bank of successes, especially in certain areas of expertise, they feel more and more confident. There are important components in here that make this one especially important.

How is the player judging their success? Recall #3 of the *Big 5* – building persistence. One of the main ideas in #3 was to help the child judge success by focusing on the *process* and doing it *relative to themselves*. Yes, this helps build persistence but it also provides the child multiple opportunities to experience success. The idea here is that if we can define success in process and self-referenced terms (get better, work hard, try hard, improve – relative to them) vs. product terms (win or lose or better than someone else) we are giving them *previous success.* Wins and beating others happen and yes it feels good but sometimes these are few and far between and based on a lot of different factors. These process, self-referenced previous successes build on each other and build and strengthen confidence.

Take home message – Previous successes are important to build a child's confidence. Let them be more about improving and learning vs. beating others...this puts more successes in the bank and builds a real base for the child. The child will in time be in games that are win/loss situations; and win some...and when they do they will love it...but when they lose they know how to persist (because of these process skills) and as a result their <u>confidence</u> is still there as they can always work at it and get after it the next time.

Verbal Persuasion – _told they can do it by a trusted source._ We likely all know how it feels when someone praises our efforts and rewards us for a task we put a lot of time into. It feels good and it gives us that little extra incentive to perhaps keep going or even know that we can keep going if we needed to. When we as parents praise our child's efforts and encourage them, it is actually building their confidence. Because they trust you, this feedback is a very important way for you to build their confidence. Of course there are specific and important ways to do this, which we cover in the next _Big 5_ component.

One thing to be aware of is giving too much or insincere verbal persuasion. Kids are savvy and smart and can learn to spot #@$ $% a mile away. In no way are we saying that there must be constant verbal persuasion but intelligently placed words do indeed build confidence.

Self perception that is accurate – _can they learn who they are?_ Cultivating an honest self-awareness is very important. We have mentioned some of these things before when we spoke of finding some players for them to watch and learn from as well as finding a direction for them to go in as a player. In addition, we discussed in concept 3 that it is important to be self-referenced vs. other references when assessing their success.

When kids learn to learn who they are they can more accurately assess how well they played relative to themselves. Sometimes kids compare themselves to other players on their team or even say, he is so good at "x" and I can't do that. But they may not need to do that. Cultivating honest self-awareness is a long journey and one that will for sure be assisted by a great coach that can help them see who they are as a player and person. But for us as parents we can help them learn how to reflect on, for instance a game or a practice, in a way that is accurate.

Also, many kids are hard on themselves when they don't need to be. The idea here is to work with them to learn how to take responsibility for the good things and the bad things they did and, because we have previously defined success as process and improvement vs. winning and beating others, the assessment of these things is self-referenced vs. other referenced. This self-referenced assessment is a good thing because they will see what they did well and work to improve and they will see what they did poorly and work to improve – both important. This accurate assessment of their own play leads to a solid foundation on which to build confidence (again, timing!)

Take home message - Developing awareness is very important, but difficult. Also, learning how to give themselves kudos for what they did well and what they need to improve on takes time but is important for improving confidence. These things take time but can bolster confidence if done right.

Styling or presenting for someone - showing someone and receiving feedback. The idea of doing something for someone frankly scares the begeebees out of a lot of people. For kids it may in fact be the same. But the truth is that kids self-present all the time for parents – when they get their clothes on, read a book, play soccer, write an essay and so on. Each of these instances is in fact an example of styling. Kids will style and present for us frequently.

When kids style in front of us it is our feedback - both verbal and nonverbal - that can make all the difference. As we will see below in the next concept, our nonverbal feedback can make all the difference in how they think they did. If we can show those little signs of "atta boys," positive head nods, smiles, good try looks, etc., this styling is an opportunity to build confidence. We will see below different ways to engage in potentialing by providing feedback - to build confidence, yes, but ultimately to build potential.

Chapter take home message - In order for us to engage in potentialing our children's confidence, we must understand that it is a long process that takes patience and time.

Confidence is built little by little. Think back to our play discussion involving scaffolding. As kids play, they have an opportunity to build their skills little by little, through small experiences that stack on each other. Think of confidence building the same way. With your assistance using the "sources of confidence" we are building these confidence roots with our children through small experiences over time. These experiences stack on each other and eventually build these deep roots in our child's confidence tree.

Notes:

_____
_____
_____
_____
_____
_____
_____
_____
_____
_____
_____
_____
_____
_____
_____
_____
_____
_____
_____
_____
_____
_____
_____
_____
_____
_____

Chapter 7 – Communication

In order to drive an environment that creates confidence, persistence and motivation, there must be communication. It truly all comes down to communication. As we communicate with our children daily, and in various ways, we must be aware of what we are saying and how we are acting relative to our child's performances. In driving the *Big 5* we must understand some basic ideas about communication.

First off though, we must not forget the glasses through which we are looking at our child's soccer. Recall at the beginning we discussed ensuring we created a place where they played soccer vs. worked soccer. Moreover, we discussed using play as a way to look at building this great environment where we were potentialing motivation, persistence and confidence. But of course to drive all 4 of these previous *Big 5* concepts we must be able to communicate efficiently and effectively.

When you think about communicating with your child think about how you like to be communicated with - and most importantly when you like to be communicated with. When you arrive home from a long mentally taxing day at work how do you like to be communicated with? Do you enjoy someone approaching you right away? Do you like some down time? Do you like to be looked at in disgust as someone shakes his or her head in disappointment? Or when you walk in the door do you like to be told that you should have done something differently at work that day and that your days work wasn't good enough? Do you like to be greeted with a hug and a "great to see you

dad/mom, hope your day was great, I am so glad you're home."
Or from your spouse, "honey, great to see you, you look
knackered, here is a beer/glass of wine." (Hey we can dream).
The point is we all like to be spoken to in different ways and at
different times – most likely in a positive supportive way.

A better analogy for us to create a picture of
communication in sport would be communication from your
child to you after a day of golf at which you played extremely
poorly and lost to players that were of far less quality than you.
You miss your last shot and your child shakes their head in
disgust. You say, "what was that for?" They say "nothing,
forget it." On the way home from the course your child is in the
back seat shaking their head, saying "I can't believe you missed
that shot to lose the last hole." "What were you thinking?"
"Why did you do so and so instead of such and such?" You
respond by saying "because _____. " They say, "that
doesn't make sense, what you should have done was
_____." You say, "lets stop to get dinner" and they say,
"let's just go home - I am disgusted you played so poorly and I
am not even hungry. I don't think I want to come watch you play
golf anymore if you are going to play like this."

A bit ridiculous? No more so than when your child has
had a tough day of soccer and your verbal feedback and
nonverbal gestures say to them – I am not proud of you and your
play today, so why bother playing? When we engage in
potentialing through communication we must be aware of types
of communication and the potential (pun intended) impact of
this communication.

Tim Howard – *Communication*

Tim Howard, as of 2012, is the Goalkeeper for The English Premier League team Everton. He is also the top choice for the US Men's National Team. Tim tells of the supportive sacrifices his mom made and the communication he had with his mother as he grew up in the game.

Esther Howard raised Tim and his brother in a one-bedroom apartment in North Brunswick, N.J., often working two jobs to cover the travel costs for all of his youth tournaments. Esther indicated that "we didn't have a lot, but love and commitment to family we had in abundance." Esther Howard indicated "it certainly wasn't easy, but the three of us were very, very close." Esther Howard spent countless hours driving Tim to his events but she looked at it as an opportunity to engage with her son. "A lot of people saw the amount of time that I spent with my children and the activities and saw that as a sacrifice.... I never did."

Tim Howard indicates that when he was young his mother gave him "lots of encouragement." Howard recollects fondly that when he was young and he was playing recreational soccer, that the other team "...would score a goal and I would start crying. I was 6 or 7. My mom would come around from the sideline to the back of the goal and tell me everything will be OK."

http://www.socceramerica.com/article/47205/tim-howards-advice-for-keepers-parents-and-coach.html

http://usatoday30.usatoday.com/sports/soccer/worldcup/2010-06-09-Howards-opportunity_N.htm

http://sports.espn.go.com/new-york/news/story?id=5300243

Defining Communication

Communication defined literally means - "the imparting or interchange of thoughts, opinions, or information by speech, writing, or signs." As we are potentialing our children we must methodically "impart" our "thoughts" via words (speech) or gestures (signs) with a clear plan to build their persistence, motivation and confidence. It is this "interchange" - of both talking and listening - that will make or break our potentialing efforts.

So where do we start? You will see below we have organized communication into 3 sections – listening, verbal feedback and nonverbal feedback. The information below is meant to get you to think about how you will communicate with your child. You will see that we have bolded a few areas to indicate that these are key areas that can impact the development of motivation, persistence, and confidence. As you go through this chapter we ask that you reflect on the previous 3 chapters and consider how you might use this information to improve motivation, persistence, and confidence. In addition, as you move to the "creating a potentialing environment" section, we ask that you consider how you might use the information there as well.

Listening

Listening is the act of hearing attentively. This indicates that we are being attentive and truly working to gather the intent of the person that is communicating with us. In fact, it has been said that the human body was gifted with two ears and one mouth for a reason.

If we are going to be effective in our potentialing we must learn to take an active approach to listen, and not just hear, what our children are truly saying and feeling.

Do you think there is a difference between hearing and listening? The difference is at the heart of potentialing. That is to say, hearing is simply the act of perceiving sound by the ear. Listening, however, is something you are consciously choosing. Listening requires concentration so that your brain processes meaning from words and behaviors.

Listening to your children requires that you are consciously paying attention to what they are trying to communicate. This is difficult as the science is to listen but the art is the timing of when/how to listen and impart knowledge. That is to say, yes we know we need to listen. But if we are to engage in potentialing we must learn the feel and timing of how to take what we have understood via our listening and turn that into meaningful feedback.

How do you know when and how to provide feedback? Really you can't know for sure, but you can have a quick rule of thumb that the goal is to decipher what they are trying to communicate. Once you learn this, it is more about what they wants vs. what you want to impart. You will then have a starting point to engage in quality verbal or nonverbal feedback with them.

Take home message – Listening is key. It is important that we listen vs. just hear – be conscious of what they are telling you. The most important rule of thumb is to get at what they want vs. what you want to get out to them.

Verbal Feedback

Verbal feedback is obviously feedback that is provided to the child from you...verbally. Much of the feedback parents deliver is corrective, focusing on improving or changing behavior. Children expect some constructive/ corrective feedback (described below), but when it is the only feedback offered, it can create a negative environment.

Most of parental feedback should be positive supportive feedback (described below) directed at the person. Remember we are supporting them in their quest to reach their potential. Sometimes the most important thing is to support the child in their sport...not the sport performance itself. A positive atmosphere motivates children to accept a challenge and risk errors or failure.

Positive feedback – are words that are encouraging. These words are the essence of building temporary and real confidence as discussed previously. When these words are imparted the impact can be immediate.

A smile, a burst of energy, and look of wow dad, thanks, I feel great now, can all be likely responses. Of course the devil is in the detail – meaning when and how much you provide this feedback is key. Too much and it becomes background music, too little and the child is left wanting. There are different types of positive verbal feedback we would like to distinguish below as they serve very different purposes.

Positive feedback about the person vs. the performance is vital. Sometimes the best thing you can say to a child, of course at the right time, is "I really enjoy watching you play." This simple statement is chalk full of goodness. It says to the child no matter what happened or happens with this game, watching you play is a great joy. It has play at the heart of the statement, and it has the soul of the child as the focus of the comment. It also says I value you above all else. Again, very powerful as often our statements are judgmental and this is not.

If performance is discussed, your lead comments regarding your child's performance should NOT be corrective (discussed below) but rather what you enjoyed about something they tried. Sometimes when you are speaking with your child, the game will come up. These are sometimes difficult situations as ultimately these should be conversations he/she should be having with the coach. But if they do come up, don't shy away from the conversation, use this as an opportunity to encourage things that they tried in the game regardless of outcome.

Remember we are building their confidence, motivation and persistence, and if we reward their attempts with our words they will see that this is what we value. This positive feedback about the attempt – regardless of outcome – is key.

As an example, perhaps the child tried a move on an opponent but failed…a few times. This move was one they were working on in training. Perhaps after the game – as a conversation organically develops about the game – this gets brought up. A simple discussion centered around "great job trying that move," that trying these in games and failing is the only way they get improved upon, focuses on the attempt vs. the outcome. This positive feedback opens the door for perhaps future discussions on things they wish they were better at during the game.

When praising a performance that the child did well, be sure to praise effort vs. ability. When a child hears you say, "wow you scored a great goal, you are a natural born soccer player," what you are praising is their ability. When a child hears you say, "wow you scored a great goal, you really worked hard to get around that defender with that move," what you are praising is their effort. This is a massive distinction and at the heart of our persistence section. When you praise the effort you are telling them this is what is most important about what you did well. When they hear this they will persist in the face of all things difficult – because they know this is what is important (effort). But when you praise the ability by saying he/she is naturally gifted, what you are really saying to the kid is that being great is what is most important.

If this is the case, then when difficulty arises, the child might protect themselves by not persisting in difficult situations for fear of failure – so he/she doesn't reach for something more but rather protects his current level of ability.

Constructive/corrective feedback – is feedback that is aimed at providing the child with information that will help them improve their behavior or game. This is a difficult one because the parent, in many cases, is not the expert in this area. For the most part this feedback should come from coaches. If it is to come from you the coaches should drive it. That is to say, if your child plays for a quality coach, there is a curriculum in place and things that are being worked on in training.

If you feel that you would like to provide your child with real information as you are talking about the game you should ask the coach what things you can say to your child in regards to the game and specifically their play. Truly though, for the most part your feedback should be positive and based on what you listened to them say to you. A danger of overusing corrective feedback is that it creates a climate where children may not want to chat or even make mistakes for fear of embarrassment or failure in the eyes of the parent.

Age plays a key factor here as well. Younger children may look for and even accept corrective feedback. The corrective feedback, if you are going to give it, should be on effort vs. quality. Remember, to build persistence we are looking to have the child focus on how hard they work vs. how great they were. So most comments from you should be relative to their work vs. their play.

Older children, if you have built a quality environment free of judgment and focused on them as a person, will engage in a conversation about their play. This is a time to let them self correct with their own feedback. As they engage you with a "what did you think of my performance" you can answer "I don't know, what did you think?" This may take some prompting with specifics about what happened where and when but the goal of the conversation is not to fix everything in the game. The goal is to have them critically and honestly think about their performance. This gives them control in the analysis and this control fosters real intrinsic motivation (choice, competence, part of your group) and confidence (perceived success).

Take home message – Positive feedback about the person is a must, it builds the person first and the performance second. Positive feedback about the performance is also good but should be focused on the effort and process vs. the ability or outcome. Finally, remember corrective feedback should mostly be for the coach as you are there for support. If you are to engage in it, the focus of the comments should come directly from the coach, focus on the process, and whenever possible take on an approach of asking the child what he or she thinks and why they think that way.

Nonverbal Feedback

Nonverbal feedback are gestures, head-shakes, eye rolls, fist pumps, etc. They are both positive and negative as well as intended and unintended.

Nonverbal feedback is effective because children usually interpret it easily and often view it as meaning more than words. The adage of a picture is worth a 1,000 words is appropriate here as sometimes no matter what you say, it is how you act that conveys the most powerful information.

Negative nonverbal feedback – **be aware!** You may have built up massive amounts of goodwill with your positive feedback only to have it undone with a poorly timed shake of the head and eye roll that sends the message "I can't believe you did that." This happens, but we must work to ensure that we minimize how often we show our displeasure. Kids watch for what we do during times that they "lay themselves on the line" during their sport. Remember, to truly get better they must really put themselves out there – it is during these times that we must be aware of how we are showing our displeasure/negative thoughts.

Positive nonverbal feedback – **believe it or fake it, but no matter what, do it.** Sometimes our kids do things on the field that we cannot believe, both for the good and the bad. When they do something for the good we likely clap, nod our heads up and down with a smile and generally express satisfaction. This for sure gets kids going and says keep doing that, it is great.

When kids do something ridiculous or poor we must work to convey a message of just keep after it, keep working, etc. Kids want to see you support them and their quest. Face it, could you do better? Not likely. Even if you are not feeling it, fake it – send the nonverbal gesture of "keep working hard" or "you can do" it by clapping for the attempt or put on the face that says "you are ok, those things happen." These are very powerful times and it is important to their confidence, motivation and persistence that they see you are on their team.

Timing. **Timing of nonverbal gestures is everything.** How are you after a game – are you welcoming with your body language or do you grab your chair and indicate "lets get the #$#$ out of here?" In the car ride – are you inviting or are you giving the old side-to-side head shake? (Depending on the age) at halftime – do you have a hug waiting for them or corrective feedback and flailing hands? These are things to think about, as remember, the goal is potentialing not conquering the world at some silly tournament on a Sunday in August.

Take home message – Nonverbal feedback is worth a 1,000 words. Negative nonverbal feedback can be detrimental in the short term – taking away their confidence in the game or in the long term - taking away their motivation to play because they feel they are disappointing you or everybody else. Positive nonverbal feedback is important and tells them you are on their team.

Section take home messages - Remember the Big 5!!!

When you are potentialing it is all about building a great environment. Yes, the content of what children are learning is important, but from your perspective as a parent the goal is to keep them excited about doing what they are doing. In order to do that, they must enjoy it – meaning play soccer vs. work soccer. Once they have this approach, then the "work hard and determination" aspect of reaching potential will be driven by them (meaning their motivation and persistence has developed). As you continue to reward them through various forms of communication for working hard and improving you will see them build this internal feeling of I can do this (temporary confidence is emerging). In time, with success and failures, they will understand what their strengths are and what they are good at and aren't good at – and each will be ok - building towards this real confidence.

Remember potentialing is not an absolute – meaning there isn't a destination that they will arrive at when they are "done." If we have focused on the process of potentialing by building this great environment, then what we have done is framed our way of thinking, possibly even changed our approach. This is the goal for you and your child. As this process unfolds, the idea is that each of you understands that potentialing is about the journey, not the destination and it is the striving to do your best that eventually leads to success – what ever that means!!

Notes:

Section 3 – Creating a Potentialing Environment

Chapter 8 – Ignition: "to arouse the passions of..."

Ok, we have all of this information, but where do we go from here? How do we assist in arousing this passion in them so that they move toward that which they can achieve? How do we help ignite this passion and desire to enjoy, improve, persist and go after something? How do we do this without shoving it down their throat and turning them off? Simple, we don't shove rather we let it happen organically.

The idea should be to inspire and provide this spark organically. We cannot ignore that our number one job in this process is to be a parent first. Meaning, yes we are potentialing BUT we are not waiting for times to crow bar confidence builders and motivation into the child every chance we get. This is for numerous reasons. The first of which is that the child will see this coming a mile away, as kids are smart about sensing something is up. Another reason is that sometimes a child just needs a parent – to talk to, hug, wipe a little blood away, etc. (We would argue that this is at the heart of potentialing as you are building their confidence in you, but back to the point). The point is that in order to be great at potentialing one needs to look at it as a process that appears seamless and methodical.

Like any good teacher, we have a lot of information that we want to share. But also like any good teacher, it cannot be given all at once – however much we want to give it all at once it is not possible and not productive.

A good teacher waits until their student is ready to receive information and then they provide them some quality tidbits of information – sometimes without them even suspecting they are learning. Little by little this teacher learner relationship takes place where the learner slowly but surely takes responsibility for their part of the learning by asking questions or initiating learning on their own. It is this slow process that allows for the learner to develop this knowledge of what and how to learn gradually…eventually leading to the desire to want to do it on their own. It is this intrinsic desire that leads to ignition, as the quest to reach their best is driven from within.

And so it is with parents and our potentialing efforts. We must understand that it is very much a slow methodical game-like process that we are engaging in with our children. Not a game in the sense of playing a trick with them but one that involves some real thoughts about making learning fun for them… making it like play. The idea is to slowly but surely bring up things here and there to engage their thinking and curiosity in the process. A program here, the talk of a great player there, followed by some genuine listening, perhaps a YouTube clip of a player or a truly heartfelt "wow, I really enjoy watching you play" are all things that can ignite that first spark of the ignition process.

In this section we lay out some ideas to help you create this potentialing environment. To get us going we discuss ideas to define your role and help you and your child set a direction in this journey. Of course these are merely suggestions, but they may help to initiate that initial spark.

Chapter 9 – Defining Your Role

Do you know what you bring to the table? Do they know what your role is in this potentialing process? The truth is, is that it is vital for parents to examine current behavior and future roles to determine how we can best assist in implanting the *Big 5*.

Lionel Messi – Roles

The winner of three consecutive European Football of the Year awards Lionel Messi had a dramatic childhood before becoming the star he is now. His father Jorge Horacio made several key decisions with and for Lionel, which resulted to be formative in his career.

Jorge encouraged his son to join his local team - Grandoli, at 5 years old. Jorge made the decision to take his son to the nearest professional team – Newell's Old Boys, when he was 8 years old, to give him a chance to shine his impressive skills. Everyday his father drove Lionel 30 miles to practice. But the important piece here is that Jorge never pushed his son into football as Lionel always wanted to train and enjoyed football.

Another fateful moment for Messi's career came when at the age of 11, he was diagnosed with a growth hormone deficiency. Jorge moved the family to Barcelona to join the youth academy of FC Barcelona. The Catalonian club not only signed the young Messi but agreed to finance the treatment of the young player's disease. Again, important in this decision was that Lionel participated in this collaborative process with his father.

Lionel Messi's father says that his contribution to his son's success is that he always supported him, didn't push him, but encouraged him to play for fun and just respected Messi's decision to dedicate his life to being a professional footballer.

http://books.google.bg/books?id=Eh8RXEwYRvcC&pg=PT6&lpg=PT6&dq=messi+grandoli+jorge&source=bl&ots=fDurlrHesg&sig=G7FRIPGJGe8hEkPfs1BdMMHQZtE&hl=en#v=snippet&q=jorge&f=false
http://en.wikipedia.org/wiki/Lionel_Messi
http://www.socceramerica.com/article/46516/messis-dad-lionel-always-played-for-fun.html

Following are two steps for you to follow in the identification of your role in this process. Interestingly, this is the shortest chapter in the book, but possibly the most important. If you can determine what your role is in the process, then you can determine much easier whether your behavior is detrimental or potentialing in nature.

Step 1 – Identify what characteristics you currently bring to the table. This is sometimes a sobering look into your behavior but necessary. What are some of your current behaviors as they relate to your child's sport? Do you know? Can you ask someone? Honestly, this is a very difficult step in this process - to look at yourself in the mirror and say what you do…it is key. Involve your kids here, as it is a real way to say to your child "I am here to improve, too, as your success is my priority."

Notes:

Step 2 – Now lets talk about roles – both yours and theirs. Yes we are talking about your role here, but there should be some bits and pieces that the player should be responsible for as well. You should begin to discuss what they think they bring to the table in terms of their role in reaching their potential. Then you should think about what you can do to help in this process of developing their potential.

Is your role to ask your child how they are feeling going into the game? Is your role to talk with your child right after the game or give him or her some space? Is your role going to be to ensure your child is focused when they are losing their focus? Honestly the best way to go about this role creation is to ask your child what he or she likes you to do and perhaps ask them if giving feedback at certain times is helpful or hurtful? This may be a very empowering moment for the child and a great way for him or her to give you access and entrance into this potentialing journey.

Notes:

Chapter take home message - To end this chapter we would like to repeat the apocryphal story of the teenager who took up snowboarding and when asked why he enjoyed it replied: "It's too cold for my parents to come and watch me snowboard and in any event they could not keep up with me. They know nothing about snowboarding so they can't provide any advice. I can enjoy myself, make mistakes and get better in a parent-free environment."

Ensure you and your child talk about and agree on your role!

Chapter 10 – Defining a Direction

What do you want for your child's soccer experience? Have you as a parent thought about it? More importantly have you and your child talked about it? Are your actions and words consistent with what you have talked about?

The truth is many of us as parents likely sign our kids up for soccer and show up to practices without giving much thought to the process...and whatever happens, happens. But think about it, would we handle school this way? Would we just show up and see what happens? Likely not. So let's ensure that we embark on our potentialing with equal methodological-ness (not a word but it's close).

This is a section on discussions with your child about soccer. The idea is to get the potentialing ball rolling. Here, you want to figure out what he or she likes about the sport and where they think they want to go. Perhaps you can share with them what you like about it as well. The most important part is to create an open dialogue that allows them to express what they think they might want.

Step 1 - Begin the "where do you want to go with this"
discussion with your child and make it organic!!!

The word organic is used here because as many of you
know, asking your child if they would like to sit down at the
kitchen table, then actually sitting down at the kitchen table to
discuss the future, is likely not going to happen. Forcing a
conversation about a child's future can sometimes be met with
"not now I'm busy" at best and sarcasm or "no chance" at worst.
Again, think methodically. We say organic because simply
bringing up conversations about the game with your child is
actually a step towards setting lifelong objectives. Here are some
ideas:

- Gradually talk about your child's game – ask him or her if
  you can talk about it. Asking first allows control on the part
  of the child. Then inserting a few of your ideas is something
  they OK'd.
- As you gradually start to talk about their game (what they
  like about it, who they sees themselves as, etc.) this will open
  up all sorts of ideas that may stimulate future conversations
  and ideas.

Notes:

Step 2 - Use the Internet with your child to identify players.

You have talked about whom your child admires / sees themselves as, why not use the web to get some more information – together. Pay attention to who the stars were as kids, where they were from, and of course what they did daily to make themselves great. Finding a great player to emulate and look up to is a great way to give your kids a picture of where they might want to go (perhaps looking at a Xavi Alonso, Alex Morgan, or Landon Donovan is far reaching, but some very good things come from looking at top players). Helpful places on the Internet include:

- Websites about individual players - these offer stories and descriptions of players as they have grown up. These stories will help the child form a picture of who the athlete is. (Examples might include: www.uefa.com / trainingground / skills / index.html, www.mlssoccer.com, www.ussoccer.com)

- Websites about teams - these offer stories and descriptions of players and their roles within their teams.

- YouTube clips about players – these offer great video of what the player has done in games.

Notes:

Step 3 - Set some time out with your child to identify just what makes these players great.

What did they do daily? What were they striving for as a youth player? Be detailed in what these players did to be great. These characteristics should be things you may value in your child in life, not just in sport. Ask your child...

- Who are their 3 favorite players?
- Why? What qualities do they identify as "good" in each player? (Note - make sure you find the right players)
- Do any of the players have any identifying mannerisms? In their play, uniform, the way they tie their boots or celebrate a goal?

Notes:

Step 4 – Have your child write down what things he or she is good at.

The player needs to know what he/she brings to the table in all of this. Help your child think about what they are good at and what they would like to improve. This is not a complete list and will not be accurate, but this is what a good coach will help with and this is a great place to start to get your child thinking.

Notes:

Take home message - Talk about what **your** **child** *enjoys about their sport and how they see themselves in the game. Make these discussions organic and just make them conversations vs. attempts at solving the world's problems!! Most of all, ensure that you begin to establish a dialogue for you and your child to discuss his or her experiences in soccer.*

Chapter 11 - Scenarios

In this section we write about some possible scenarios that may take place between you and your child. These scenarios set forth times where you might be able to apply information learned about in the *Big 5* or information defined by you and your son/daughter in the roles and direction chapters.

Car Rides

The Car Ride To Practice

The car ride to practice can be a time where lots of things happen. This is a chance to allow your child to talk about their day and desires. Depending on the amount of time it takes to get to practice, they may be able to share their mood going into training.

Our suggestion - The goal for you here is listening to what they think about their sessions. As you drive to practice, perhaps ask them what they are looking forward to most about practice. They will likely say scrimmaging. Ask them what they then think is most difficult about practice. This may give you some insight about what they feel like they might fail at – key in on this. The reason is that it is during these times of un-comfort when they will need you the most as they move forward.

@ You may have a different perspective on this or wish to read other examples of this scenario. Please visit www.potentialing.com to interact with others and read additional ideas.

The Car Ride Home From Practice And Games

The car ride home has a lot of elements as well. Tired and hungry kids are usually the norm. When kids get in the car they frequently do not want to talk about training or games. They want to giggle with their friends, listen to music, etc. They are ready to do something else. Remember they have just worked hard for 60-90 minutes, so by this time they should be spent.

The goal here is to <u>listen</u> and just be there! Depending on how tired they are, what they really want to hear is what is for dinner. Sometimes building persistence is best accomplished by doing nothing at all. Remember – this is their safe place. Let them get in the car and chill out. Ask them if they had fun. If they engage, ask them what was fun about it. Respond with a "yes, that looked cool" type of response – perhaps even a complement that you saw them try something during that exercise...focus your responses on play.

The time to talk about what they did well or could have done better is not right away. Remember no crowbarring. Wait until the child has had a chance to decompress and then perhaps talk about something you saw them do well. If they bite, see what they thought about it. If they don't, then leave it alone. We repeat - leave it alone!!! The potentialing process is sometimes better left alone!!! Again, visit www.potentialing.com if you have or want to read others different experiences.

The car ride to games is usually filled with excitement....but sometimes not. If a child is feeling confident they will frequently show it in their behavior - behaving in their normal way chatting it up, listening to music, etc. If they are not confident – if perhaps they are not feeling like they are ready - they will engage in behaviors out of the norm.

Watch, listen and be there. The idea here is truly to watch their behavior. Sometimes the best things you can do are to say nothing and gauge their mood.

Confidence building is also really at play here. Dr. Hancock and Robin Russell share unique perspectives on how to build confidence during car rides. For additional ideas on how to build children's confidence in car ride scenarios, please visit www.potentialing.com.

Meals

Breakfast

Breakfast is truly the most important meal of the day. Yes because of the food that is served up but mostly because of the conversation that can be served up. Potentialing is about finding these key times to be around for your son or daughter. Breakfast is a time where they are first engaging in the day, and in many households, the meal is rushed. But moving quickly doesn't mean moving carelessly. Slipping in a word here and a word there is what it is all about.

The *Big 5* are all at play here. Perhaps it is breakfast on game day and the child is chatty – easy – participate in the excitement of the day by going with the flow. Perhaps your child is saying they are anxious about playing a new position...this is a chance at building persistence or confidence by talking about it as an opportunity vs. not. Perhaps your son or daughter is worried about a test that day and not even thinking about sports....great...motivation, persistence and confidence are at play here too – listen, remember the important factors in building each and empower that kiddo.

Dinner

Dinner is not always a stagnant thing – sometimes it is done on the road or in a restaurant. Whatever the case may be the point is that the time and location for dinners of soccer parents usually only have one consistent thing – it involves you and them and some sort of food item. Dinner is a time where the day and the sport have usually caught up to a child and they are knackered. They need food, some love and relationship time now.

Yes, listening to them and building the *Big 5* can happen here, but sometimes this is a good place to insert a story or two about you. Some of the best learning experiences that kids can have is when they learn about you and your triumphs and struggles. Now may be a good time to engage in potentialing by taking some things they are going through and weaving them harmlessly into something that happed to you….and talk about how perhaps you had to work hard/try hard etc., how you had to work through it, and how you look back and feel fortunate to have gone through that experience. These conversations can be a lot of fun and of course there is some learning going on as well.

@

Meal times for soccer families are sometimes crazy and unpredictable. Visit us at www.potentialing.com to share your "unique" interactions and attempts at potentialing during meal times.

Games

Game Days

It would be a good start to ask your child how they would like you to support them on Game Days: before the game, during the game and after the game. Decide what you as parents can realistically affect e.g., how much rest and sleep, how we will get there, what might be for lunch, etc. Be sure their playing gear and footwear are ready. It may also be worthwhile asking your child what they DON'T want you to do on game days, e.g. talk to them while they are trying to play and criticize them and their teammates.

During The Game

In game behavior is vital. This is a massive opportunity to engage in potentialing. Your head nods, words, arm actions and any other verbal or nonverbal gestures make a big impression on your son or daughter. Hopefully your child does not look over to you for approval every time they perform something in a game. Truthfully, if they do, it is usually a sign that they are seeking approval for everything they do...which is not good.

Your number one job is to encourage them with your behavior and with your words. Yes they will make some ridiculous choices with and without the ball. Yes the ball will come flying off of their feet in lots of different directions. Sometimes they will not even be working hard. Yes, this is all normal and part of the game, and you do not need to be the coach and correct them or judge them. These are sometimes quite frustrating experiences but it is important to remember back to the section on communication about what makes an impression and why it makes an impression.

In the game, encourage them with your behavior and words. Praise their attempts. When they make a mistake, think about ways to encourage them to work hard to get up and get at it again.

Games and game days are unique and dependent on a number of factors including things such as ages of the children involved, times of games, and perceived pressure by the athletes (and parents). We invite you to share your experiences with these scenarios as well as view other parents' experiences at www.sportspath.com.

You can also log in with your password to access Soccer Parent Course 3 at www.sportspath.com and view Module 2 to review the ways you support your child on Game Day.

Sometimes watching a soccer game on TV is just about watching a game on TV. But this is also a big opportunity to engage in potentialing using components from the *Big 5*. There are a number of things that can be talked about during this time. From how the team is playing, to what a specific player is about, from how a player might feel after making a bad mistake to what impact a substitute may have and how hard a player has worked to come back from injury.

Watching a game you will find all the elements of the *Big 5* at play. You will see players that truly look like they love playing the game. Talk about those players and how hard they work and how much they seem to enjoy this work. You will see players that make those big mistakes and you can talk about how that might affect their confidence and how that confidence, or lack thereof, shows itself in the game. You will see a player persist in the face of very difficult circumstances – perhaps on the road in the second leg of a home and away series where they are down 2-1 on aggregate. Focus on the process as it is one goal at a time vs. win, win, win.

@

However you want to handle watching a game with your child, just do it. Don't feel like you need to comment on everything - sometimes it's just about watching some great players play. Visit www.sportspath.com to share your unique viewing experiences.

Success and Failure

Dealing With Success

Sometimes you may find yourself with a child that experiences a lot of early success. They win trophies with their club teams, individual accolades, and overall praise for being a good player. Remember - we are potentialing and potentialing is a process with no endpoint.

The goal for us as potentialing parents is to understand that first and foremost that it is OK that the child has early success. It is OK that they win games, individual accolades and praise. However, they should understand why they are receiving this praise and understand that success and potentialing is limitless and a process, and early success doesn't ensure success later in life.

Perhaps they are receiving this success because they are bigger, stronger and faster? If this is the case, these attributes have very little to do with soccer prowess and a lot to do with genetics – which often impacts early success. Again it is OK to have this early success but they must constantly look to be improving in areas that are going to make them better everyday, not just rest on their God given abilities.

OK, so now how do we deal with those failures that will for sure happen? What happens when a player does not make a team? Or a player does not earn a game ball that they felt they earned? Or makes a mistake that appears to cost their team a victory? All these things and more will happen to our children along the way in soccer...so what to do?

Failures are times to gain valuable experience. Think about it, we as adults have probably learned as much or more from our difficult experiences as we have from our successes. Failure is a part of sports and as such gives us plenty of opportunities as potentialing parents to help our kids see the value in these times.

So, the first thing we need to do as potentialing parents is embrace failure as an opportunity, not shove it aside and not deal with it. Too often people make a mistake or don't earn something they thought they'd earned and then refuse to deal with it because it is too painful to think about. This helps nothing. Embrace this idea of failure and talk about it in terms of learning experiences as opposed to times of shame and embarrassment. This will help kids reframe it in terms of the process of potentialing vs. the product of winning or being the best. Yes, it's nice to do both, but that comes with time and practice.

Dr. Hancock and Robin Russell have had a lot of opportunities to work with athletes of all ages that experience many successes and failures. For our unique perspective, as well as others ideas and suggestions on how to use the *Big 5* in these situations, visit www.sportspath.com. We understand that what works with one child may not work with another child. This is why we invite you to read what others have encountered when they applied the ideas in our book. In addition, we invite you to post (anonymously if you wish) what may have happened in your situation when working on potentialing with your child. We hope you will also share additional scenarios *not* identified in our book. It is our goal to create a supportive community of parents working at potentialing with their kids.

Remember to use your password to log in to www.sportspath.com to access Soccer Parent Course 2 Module 3 for some practical advice on approaching the coach. Access Course 3 Module 3 to review the ways you can provide support through setbacks and successes.

Section 4

Selecting and Ensuring a Potentialing Environment

Chapter 12 - Selecting a Soccer Program

This section provides some nuts and bolts that we feel can help you ensure that you are selecting and ensuring a potentialing environment for your child. In particular this chapter focuses on finding a quality coach and club for your child. Choosing a quality teacher and classroom is vital and so too the single most important decision for the parent to make in terms of potentialing their child through sport is to choose a soccer club/team and ensure a quality coach for their child.

It would be appropriate for parents to consider how much time and effort they put into choosing a new car, washing machine, TV or sound system against the time they take to choose a youth soccer club for their children and evaluate the coaches at the club. In reviewing the choices that parents need to make, there are normally a number of decisions at various ages.

It is worth noting that studies of player development programs throughout the world have indicated that clubs with a commitment to individual personal development provide the best results in not only developing elite players but in having a low percentage of drop outs. Such clubs emphasize these factors:

- High levels of time devoted to *practice*: recommending at least 3 practice sessions to one game. This is the most important single factor in improvement. Practice makes permanent. As we know in so many fields, time spent practicing will be a key factor. Practice at home, in the back yard, with your child's friends and at a club.
- Access to *good coaches*: your children will be spending a lot of time with the coaches, and these individuals will have a significant impact on your children.
- An 'appropriate' *games program*: games by themselves simply don't provide the repetition to practice skills.

Choosing a Program

These days the majority of programs that develop soccer players in the US and Europe are soccer clubs. There are for sure other places to develop as a player, such as local leagues / gaming circuits with teams, school based programs, etc. While these other options do exist, the majority of quality places for kids to develop their soccer skills are in clubs.

Choosing a club is a very important step in ensuring a potentialing environment extends beyond you. No matter where you live you should have high expectations of where your son or daughter will develop. Perhaps in your community there are limited choices of youth soccer clubs or perhaps there are many.

It doesn't matter how many options you have, you should have expectations of what the club offers.

Below we recommend a list of factors you should look for when choosing a club. It's not to say all of these things exist, but you should consider a number of these as you select a place for him/her to develop.

The club has stated values - This indicates the club has a vision and wishes to pursue policies to achieve them. Are these values compatible with yours? As a family you will have decided certain family values so it is reasonable to assume you would like to ensure that the soccer club you choose for your child is compatible with these family values. No amount of input from you, the parents, will compensate for a poor club, which does not reinforce your family values.

The club is a club and not just a collection of teams. Some clubs you will find are just a collection of teams that show up to train but have little connection to each other. However, a proper club will have a director of coaching and teams that no know one another, may play or train with one another, and generally not just coexist but rather utilize each other to move forward in the development process. This is made easier by the fact that coaches know each other and work well together.

The club is communicative. You should expect communication from the club regarding issues ranging from current goings on to alumni news to information on when practice fields are open or closed. While sometimes this information comes from your coach, if you have a cohesive club this news should also come from the club itself.

The club ensures its teams train on quality fields. A player cannot develop properly if the physical environment at which they are training is not of quality. The field should generally be free from holes and should be grass or field turf. Yes, sometimes there is long grass and divots here and there but it is vital that a playing surface is playable or a child cannot develop. The lighting should be adequate as well. Players can get injured if they cannot see when they are training. The team should have enough space to train. Frequently many teams practice at the same time. This is fine as long as there is ample space for the coach to conduct exercises he/she needs to properly develop the players.

The club has qualified staff. Good clubs have quality coaches from top to bottom (see next chapter for what makes a quality coach). This is important because there will be a time in a good club where the team is passed to a different coach or a player is placed on a different team. This should not be an issue if the quality of the staff is good overall.

The club makes a commitment to individual development. This is vital, as players must develop individually in the team environment. While practices should for sure have an element of individual development, the club should provide an opportunity to develop the individual by offering a skills night, position specific trainings, or skills development program.

The club has programs that develop the whole person. Players are not just players, but they are also students and developing young adults. As such, they require more than just soccer training. Elite soccer programs provide additional trainings for players in areas such as college preparation, nutrition guidance, physiological trainings, or life skills training sessions. While these are not programs that every club has, if you can find one, it sure does help.

The club provides an opportunity to play up or with other teams within the club. If it is truly a club, then the coaches will know players within the club and talk about those players. There should be an opportunity, if the player deserves it, to move up or guest with a team within the club. This is an important opportunity for those players wishing for and needing a challenge.

The club is committed to providing oral or written feedback to the parent and player. You should have an expectation that your child is developing. To this end, quality clubs ensure their coaches provide feedback, whether written or spoken, to members and their children about this development.

The club has an appropriate games program. Games are an examination of progress. Games may have limited practice value if the player is not close to the action and the ball! A quality games program ensures that the appropriate number of players per age range are involved in the game (4v4 for U-5 to U-7; 8v8 for U-8 to U-10; 11v11 for U-11 to U-18 {although this is still too many}). Players are provided ample opportunities to play. While this does not mean playing time is equal, you should have an expectation that your child will play a good amount of time in most games. The focus of the games is on development. While there is nothing wrong with winning, it is a byproduct of quality development.

Opting for an 'Elite Program'

What if you want to consider enrolling your child in an 'elite program?' The considerations are similar to choosing a club, but the time commitment and opportunities are greater, as are indeed the risks. In the United States there are a number of elite program options that parents should be aware of as they choose the right place for their child to develop. How can you know if your child is ready for this level of soccer?

Truly, deciding if your son or daughter is ready for the next level of soccer is a difficult question to answer. The best way to do it is ask trusted professionals in the field. If you know a coach or someone familiar with the landscape of club soccer, ask them. If not, you may refer to a resource from the Soccer Parent Course 4 at www.sportspath.com and view Module 1.

Other Resources

As mentioned previously, our Soccer Parent Course at www.sportspath.com provides additional information relative to choosing a best place for your son or daughter to ensure they are reaching their potential. Apart from the information it provides in choosing an elite club that is right for your child, it also provides information on ways to select places for your younger, emerging players to best develop. Below are some suggestions:

- At approximately 4 years of age your child may be ready for a soccer day camp or recreational soccer. There are many great organizations throughout the country in this category. See course 2 at www.sportspath.com to assist you.

- At approximately 6 or 7 years of age, a great place for your child to develop could be at the recreational level or club level – depending on a number of factors. See course 2 at www.sportspath.com to assist you.

- At approximately 9 or 10 years of age your child may be ready for a competitive travel club team. See course 3 at www.sportspath.com to assist you.

- At approximately 13 years of age your child may be ready for an elite team. See course 4 at www.sportspath.com to assist you.

Chapter 13 – Choosing a Coach

The best youth soccer clubs in the world have coaches who love coaching kids. They have an understanding of their needs. Steve Heighway, the former Liverpool FC player and Director of their Academy said that he thought the major characteristic he looked for in coaches of young players was that they "knew more about children than soccer." To this end we have compiled a list of things you should look for when selecting a good coach for your child.

What are the characteristics of good coaches?

They are good people. Face it, would you want a sleazeball coaching your child? Likely answer – no. But if you look into the background of some of the supposed "good" coaches out there, that is just what you will find - a person that does not handle themselves away from the field in an ethical manner. Sometimes it seems as if parents are willing to look the other way just because they may be improving their child's skill set. But the question you should be asking yourself is – is this a quality role model? OR, is this person teaching my son or daughter life lessons?

You have every right to watch the coach and how he/she behaves off the field. The best way to learn about a person is to watch him or her when they do not know you are watching.

In addition, ask people you trust and who might be in the know about the coach and how he chooses to spend his free time. I am not saying he/she needs to be an angel, however, you should have certain expectations of someone that your child is spending so much time with.

They are qualified with children. It is important to understand children, as coaches teach children, they do not teach soccer. That is to say while the content is of course important, it is the understanding of the child that is vital to ensure the information gets taught. To this end it is important that coaches have a background in educating children.

There are many ways that someone can gain insight into developing children. Perhaps the coach has a college education with some sort of teaching background. Perhaps he/she has been around a number of children throughout their life and understands how they develop. Perhaps they have been around good coaches and understand the logical progression in teaching kids. Whatever qualification, the idea is that the person should have some qualification or experience in developing children.

They are qualified as coaches. The coaches at the club may or may not have been good players but **all** coaches have relevant, current, qualifications. You wouldn't let your child in a car with an unqualified driver, so surely a qualified coach for your child is a must.

US Soccer has licenses for coaches. The licenses range from National A licenses (the highest license in the country) to State E licenses. See www.ussoccer.com/coaches/licenses.aspx for more details on licenses, what they mean and what coaches have to go through to earn them.

In addition, other entities both nationally and internationally provide licenses and diplomas. The NSCAA has licenses and certificate education programs that indicate a coach has met certain requirements as a coach (www.nscaa.com/education/courses). In addition, a license that you will frequently see is a UEFA sanctioned license. UEFA is the governing board for soccer in Europe and grants licenses that are difficult to obtain which usually indicate a qualified individual (www.uefa.com).

What do good coaches do well?

Good coaches have qualities that you can recognize as things that are helpful in developing your kids. These qualities obviously involve being a good person, being good with children and being qualified. But these qualities manifest themselves in what they do day in and day out. To help you select a coach, we have made a list of things good coaches do well – frequently.

Good coaches create an environment that kids enjoy. We spent a good portion of the book talking about the importance of a great environment.

It makes sense then that we would do the same here as it relates to coaches. Good coaches create an environment that kids want to come to. They make it challenging, fun, engaging and above all else, a place where the child feels safe. Find this environment and you have found a great place for your child to develop.

Good coaches are enthusiastic. Enthusiasm galvanizes and is infectious - pessimism paralyzes! Every age group needs energy. Little ones often need big energy and boisterousness to ensure the group is excited about the task at hand. Moreover, if the coach of little ones has passion, this is often passed down to the players. Older ones also need enthusiasm. Perhaps the enthusiasm here is the passion for the game and the way they show up every day ready and organized to do work. While every team needs something different, all good coaches show a passion for the game.

Good coaches know the kids. If you show up for training and the coach knows your son/daughters name, that is a good thing. When the coach also knows a few personal things about your child and asks questions to your child about how they are doing in so and so and what are your grades in math class, etc., it shows that he/she is interested in what is going on with the child as a person. The other piece of this is that if the coach knows about the child, then he is paying attention to the little things that the player does well and what makes them tick. This is important given that the child will struggle at some point and the coach will need to know how to help that child as an individual.

Good coaches are good teachers. As you watch a great coach run a session, it is very much like how a great teacher runs a classroom. He/she is organized, he/she develops the session in a logical progression, he/she gives quality coaching points relative to the topic of the day and generally provides information that will help your child develop their skills. As opposed to coaches that just throw out the ball and let the session run itself. Also, when you watch a coach coach in a game, is he/she screaming up and down the sideline without any sense of the things worked on in training? Or, is he/she providing feedback, relative to the ideas provided in training, and in a positive supportive way?

Good coaches provide good feedback. The coach does not overly interrupt the session but when the coach does intervene the coach is providing quality information so that the player can improve and develop. The coach may shout, whisper or use a whistle - they key aspect is whether the coach holds the attention of the group. Does the coach concentrate on praising the effort of ability? Remember – it is critical to focus on effort over ability.

Good coaches develop thinking players. Good coaches ask that players show up to training to work hard but also show up to training to think. They create exercises and expectations where players are asked to solve developmentally appropriate problems.

These exercises and expectations will help develop these skills so that players can do these in games, at a low level now and at a higher level when they are older.

While this list is not exhaustive, it is a place to start. Finding the right coach is truly important as they will shape how your child develops as well as how they see and enjoy the game overall.

Chapter 14 – Additional Potentialing Ideas for Parents

There are many things parents can do to provide their children additional opportunities to develop and also just enjoy the game. Below we provide a few ideas for you to do with and for your children. Since we realize this list only scratches the surface, we invite you to share additional ideas at www.potentialing.com.

Playing soccer with your kids. A great way to be able to "get in the door with them" so to speak is to simply go outside and knock it around with them. It is so simple, but a huge way to make an impact on them. Obviously at the younger ages this is easy as kids frequently ask if they can play with you. Do it. Take the time to put down what you are doing and pass the ball, kick it against the wall, play one on one or simply do something with them involving the ball. At the older ages this probably happens less frequently but perhaps you can offer to see if they want you to play, pick up so and so, and head to the park.

Encouraging pick-up games. Kids simply need to play more soccer, on their own. If you can encourage this by purchasing small goals, taking them to the park, offering to pick up a friend or setting up small fields in your backyard, this can go a long way in their development. Offer up plenty of opportunities for this to happen but of course get them to choose doing it or it becomes forced – which is never a good thing.

Challenging them to use their imagination in their pickup games. Young children have an enormous capacity for make believe and imagination. To re-enforce the 'PLAY' aspect of the potentialing skills, without attempting to coach your child – when they are next playing pick-up games, add to the excitement of the activities by feeding this imagination and asking them some of the following questions.

- Who are you today? How can I tell that (he/she needs to point out some key mannerisms)?
- What will be a part of your game I should notice?
- Which team are you on? Which other players are there? Which field or stadium?
- What's the score?

You can further add to the enjoyment of the pick-up games your child plays with their friends by printing off Fantasy Game Cards at www.potentialing.com. Sports Path ™ Fantasy Game Cards are best used for children aged 8 – 14 years of age and encourages them to discuss tactics, agree action and improve their game understanding. They can be used for any game of 3-aside or more. You can of course devise your own challenges but children do react well if the tasks are in written form and especially if you can place them in sealed envelopes for them to open.

To use them:

- Print off a Card for each team to view
- Give the team about 3 minutes to agree their tactics and strategy
- Let the game commence for a short defined period (10-15 minutes)
- Discuss after the game the success of the team's tactics and strategy

Playing some back yard (non soccer) games. Without coaching your child encourage them as much as possible to play games that involve changing direction, speed and trickery. Try some of these ideas:

- www.gameskidsplay.net/games/chasing_games/index.htm.
- Let the children make up their own games with their own rules, which they need to referee themselves.
- In games, try to highlight things like the need for all players to cooperate in order to solve problems, try to win fairly, respect the opponent, and respect the rules of the game (that hopefully they set).

Watching games on TV with your kids. Again, so simple but do you do it? We bring this up in the scenarios section but it's worth bringing up here again as many people talk about soccer with their kids but do not actually watch it on TV. Watching TV serves many different purposes.

First and foremost it is an opportunity for you to bond with your child over a sporting event...always fun.

This game watching can really be something you start together, as perhaps neither of you have a favorite team...and you can find one together. This is also an opportunity to find players that your child likes/feels like they relate to. This is a powerful motivator and also very educational as he or she can see what they do to impact the game. Finally it is a time to talk about how these players got to where they are. Recall above the Henrik Larson story - sometimes it all starts with a single glimpse and conversation about a player or team.

Videoing and photographing your child playing soccer. Use the camera on your mobile phone to capture good examples of your child playing soccer. Develop an album of still photographs and video clips of your child so they can view these online or print them into their own skills diary. These can be great motivational and educational aids for your child.

When filming try to concentrate on specific aspects such as the following: key techniques when your child is in possession of the ball (e.g. turning dribbling, shooting, passing), moments when your child is not in possession of the ball, moments when his/her team loses possession of the ball (do they move towards to the ball to deny space to opponents?), or when his/her team gains possession of the ball (do they move away from the ball to look for space)?

For additional ideas on potentialing activities, and/or to submit an idea, please visit www.potentialing.com.

Quick ending...which is hopefully the beginning

Hopefully as you have read this book you have picked up some little gems that you have already used with your child. For us, the goal was always to provide you with ideas on ways you might help your son or daughter realize who they can become. While we understand this is a long journey filled with many uncertainties, we also realize the more you know, the more you can be a part of potentialing their possible skills and abilities.

Potentialing is a deliberate act but hopefully we have shown that it is part doing and part not doing. Meaning sometimes parents provide information or assistance and sometimes we are simply there for our child. Hopefully we have made our case for the *Big 5* - that using the *medium* of Play and the *skills* of Communication drives forward your child's Confidence, Persistence and Motivation.

We hope our relationship does not end here. We understand that parents are constantly learning, as are we as authors and professionals. Which is why we would like to be of continued help and service through our blogs, e-learning courses and workshops.

As a reminder:

- To access our blogs and continue to provide us and other parents and coaches quality scenarios and potentialing ideas, please visit www.potentialing.com.
- If you are interested in scheduling a workshop or guest speaker appearance for your team, club or organization, please visit www.potentialing.com to explore some options.
- If you would like to enroll in the e-learning courses as part of the purchase of this book please visit www.sportspath.com.

We realize that a parent's job is about, well, parenting. But of course we also believe parenting is about potentialing^{TM}. Enjoy the journey!

Acknowledgements

From Lee Hancock

I would like to thank my parents for all of their potentialing efforts. I would like to thank my wife Rachel - you are an understanding and patient spouse and world-class mom. To my sons Jaden, Gavin, and Owen, I love you very much. You are great boys and I truly do enjoy watching you play. I have said to each of you often that I believe my most important job in life is to be a good dad...hopefully you feel as you grow that I am doing/have done a good job.

From Robin Russell

I would like to thank my wife, Adrienne, for her patience, my late parents – Gladys and Dave Russell - for their influence as such role models for me and especially I would like to thank Skype – as Lee and I would not have been able to progress this book without free video calls.

19368192R00073

Made in the USA
Lexington, KY
18 December 2012